Praying to the God of Small Things

Praying to the God of Small Things

Poems by

Catherine Jagoe

© 2024 Catherine Jagoe. All rights reserved.
This material may not be reproduced in any form, published,
reprinted, recorded, performed, broadcast,
rewritten, or redistributed without
the explicit permission of Catherine Jagoe.
All such actions are strictly prohibited by law.

Cover design by Shay Culligan
Cover artwork by Holly Knott (HollyKnott.com)
—"The Lafayette Sycamore"
Insect photographs by Mike McDowell

ISBN: 978-1-63980-557-0

Kelsay Books
502 South 1040 East, A-119
American Fork, Utah 84003
Kelsaybooks.com

For Nickole

Acknowledgments

Many thanks to the journals where the following poems first appeared, sometimes in earlier versions:

About Place Journal: "The Cailleach at Twelve Below," "Acorn Weevil," "Hornworm"
Boomer Lit: "First Anniversary," "Mayday Manifesto"
Canary: A Literary Journal of the Environmental Crisis: "Triptych"
Peninsula Pulse: "Oracle," "Things I Learned This Month"
The Plant-Human Quarterly: "Praise Song for a Plane Tree"
Salzburg Poetry Review: "Memento Mori," "No Matter How Full"
Wisconsin Academy Review: "Maple in October"

Thank you also to the editors of the anthologies and publications where the following poems previously appeared:

Echolocations: Poets Map Madison edited by Sarah Busse, Shoshauna Shy, and Wendy Vardaman (Cowfeather Press, 2013): "Epitaphs"
News from the North (Finishing Line Press, 2014): "Dog on the Median of the Kennedy Expressway, Chicago," "Still, Life"
Poetry Walk, Stevens Point, Wis. (April 2024): "Good Friday in the Department of Natural Resources"
Where the Grass Still Sings: Stories of Insects and Interconnection by Heather Swan (Penn State University Press, 2024): "Cherry Faced Meadowhawk"
Wisconsin Poets' Calendar and Wisconsin Public Radio: "Honey"

"Dog on the Median" was set to music by composer Jasper Wald and premiered by Madison Chamber Choir in May 2017.

Selected words from Aldo Leopold's essay "On a Monument to the Pigeon" from *A Sand County Almanac* appear in my erasure poem of the same title by kind permission of the Aldo Leopold Foundation, for which I am very grateful.

Warmest thanks to Mike McDowell for sharing his expertise as a birder and entomologist and for allowing me to include some of his insect photographs, which inspired most of the poems in Part II.

Likewise, to Holly Knott for allowing me to include an image of her quilt art on the front cover, which shows the famous Lafayette Sycamore in Pennsylvania, a tree that was likely growing in 1682 when William Penn founded the state.

"Praise Song for a Plane Tree" and "Sermon from the Marsh" would not exist without extraordinary poet and writing teacher Nickole Brown and her "Kingdom of Green" and "Kingdom Animalia" workshops.

Boundless gratitude to the gifted writers in my poetry critique group: Alison Townsend, Robin Chapman, Jesse Lee Kercheval, Sara Parrell, Rita Mae Reese, Marilyn Annucci, and Anne-Marie Cusac, who read and discussed versions of these poems as they came into being.

To Heather Swan, for full-moon walks and talks and for sharing her wide-ranging knowledge and love for insects, art, poetry, and the natural world.

To Lynn Keller, former director of the Center for Culture, History, and Environment at the University of Wisconsin-Madison, for wonderful ecopoetry book recommendations and our visits to the International Crane Foundation.

To Christy and Jack, for taking me to Indian Ford Meadow.

To Lisa Fishman for inspiration and heirloom apples.

To the artist residencies at Write On, Door County in Wisconsin, PLAYA in Oregon, the Virginia Center for the Creative Arts, and Jentel in Wyoming, where some of these poems first germinated.

Lastly, I wrote the title poem, "Praying to the God of Small Things," without conscious reference to Arundhati Roy's 1997 novel *The God of Small Things,* but I would be remiss if I did not acknowledge it and thank her for imagining such a god.

Contents

I

Something Like History	19
At Ten	20
Oracle	21
Dog on the Median of the Kennedy Expressway, Chicago	22
Things I Learned This Month	23
The Cailleach at Twelve Below	24
First Anniversary	26
Epitaphs	27
Still, Life	28
Good Friday in the Department of Natural Resources	30
Mayday Manifesto	31
Vouchsafed	33
Postcard from Washington Island, Wisconsin	34
Maple in October	35
It is December and we must be brave	36
Aldo Leopold's "On a Monument to the Pigeon": An Erasure	38
Disappearing the Birds	41
Unseasonable	43
Sermon from the Marsh	44

II

The Naturalist, July 2020	49
The Lovers	51
Green, I Love You Green	53
Nymph	55

Hornworm	57
Stowaway	59
Cherry-Faced Meadowhawk	61
Cicadas	63
Peacock Fly	65
Leafhopper Search	67
Acorn Weevil	69
Praying to the God of Small Things	71
Whisper, Universe, Eclipse	74
The Fog Harvesters	76

III

Desert Soliloquy	83
Thanksgiving at Indian Ford Meadow	84
Four Collects	85
Self-Portrait as Yellow Warbler	86
No Matter How Full	88
Empty Nest Ghazal	89
Wisconsin Honey	90
Dance Floor	91
Schoolhouse Beach, Washington Island, Wisconsin	92
Triptych: A Book of Hours	93
Fish Out of Water	95
Memento Mori	96
To Have But Not to Hold	98
Praise Song for a Plane Tree	100

Notes

The small of the world loom large.
Russian proverb

*Let them not say: we did not see it.
We saw.*
Jane Hirschfield

We must risk delight.
Jack Gilbert

I

Something Like History

Mother was the sun with an on/off switch.
Father held a tarantula close to his heart.

He sired me on a continent of crumbling empires.
We knew other ghosts and lordlings just like us.

Then we moved Back Home, where everything
was grey. Grey's dirty dishcloth

wiped out all the light that came before;
England a cramped and dingy place

of low horizons and a basement witch,
doors and faces slamming shut.

"Liar," the white kids said. "You can't
be from Africa. You're not Black."

I made friends with moss, its tiny forests
on the brick wall, stared at them for hours,

learned belonging from the soft,
sweet, indefatigably patient grass.

At Ten

Lumpy, earnest and short-sighted,
often it was only the small that consoled me
in those years of schoolyard cruelties—
things I could get close to.
The freckled throats of foxgloves.
Snapdragons' soft jaws. Liverwort
on the stream bank, oozing
and slippery with life. Birch bark curls
where I'd inscribe a favorite word—
moonstone, say, or *rosehip, tendril.*
Tadpoles sprouting limbs, graceless
and strange as my own expanding,
elongating body with its bracken-
stained knees. The crushable nubs
of pineapple weed in pavement
cracks, and bluebells in the woods,
their scent a music, every stem
bent by the weight of tiny bells
whose wild, sweet witchery
still haunts me. And one day
that most pedestrian of miracles:
donning the ugly, dreaded glasses—
government-issued, brown plastic—
and the wonderment of seeing
every single tree had leaves.

Oracle

Once, as a teen, I asked a man
on the street if he had the time.

"No," he replied. "But I have
the record of its passing."

It was a grey day, on a grimy street
in a small provincial town.

I was on my way to the dentist,
fretting I might be late.

He was an older man,
in a suit of some kind,

a little formal, but not memorable—
tweed, or perhaps a trench coat.

I never did learn the time.
I have never forgotten.

I mention this in the same way
certain things loom out at you

when you're on a bike
and pedaling hard, focused,

and afterwards all you remember
are instants, imprinted: a killdeer

on the shoulder, feigning a broken wing,
a hillside covered in sweet clover,

or the small, round hole in the road
that could have thrown you.

Dog on the Median of the Kennedy Expressway, Chicago

I keep coming back
to that dog
running west
next to the fast lane
along the concrete meridian
between eight
lanes of traffic

and wishing
I could have stopped
although it was impossible
four lanes of us
nose to tail
seventy miles an hour

that dog, thin, grey,
loping doggedly along
no Samaritan in sight
nowhere to go but on

Things I Learned This Month

after William Stafford

Honeybees point their hivemates toward food,
dancing to communicate direction, distance.

A sunflower's heart is made of thousands
of miniature florets inside its petalled disk.

When a stroke stilled Tranströmer's right hand,
he taught himself to play piano with the left.

The builders of Stonehenge and other Neolithic
monuments were probably just teenagers.

Sixty years after the first aircraft stayed aloft for just
three seconds, astronauts were orbiting the earth.

The human eye relaxes when gazing at distant objects
and finds the color green most restful.

After a factory accident left him briefly blind,
John Muir went on a thousand-mile walk.

Male blue whales can sing for hours or days
to others hundreds of miles away.

Ice has an entire sonic repertoire—it can sound
like gunshots, or music from another world.

The Cailleach at Twelve Below

*In Gaelic mythology, the Cailleach
is the crone-goddess of winter and wild things*

All morning the Cooper's hawk
has been slaking the hunger
that harrows her—a house finch
seized from the feeder.

All morning hunched at her
work under the arborvitae
she takes her sweet
time to gralloch him,

too small but all she could cull.
She wields her billhook,
plucking, rending, tugging,
prying tendon from bone,

the frigid yard devoid
of birds save one mourning
dove, watching, knowing
he's safe while she

unseams her pinioned
prey and loots its rubies,
pecks the tongue from the slack
beak, then the soft dull eye-

berries, splits the wish-
bone, yanks back the matchstick
rack, the treasure-chest
lid of the numbles—

heart, spleen, crop still full
of sunflower seed, gizzard,
kidney, liver, lights,
the pinworm roil of guts—

leaving, when she leaves,
just a rickle of feathers,
not even a trace
of blood on the snow.

First Anniversary

after W. S. Merwin

This week, without knowing it, I passed the day
my last blood came to me,
all flood and bloat and ache,
flush with imperatives.
I will no longer mimic
the moon and tides,
the pearl in oyster flesh.
My womb's retired and a certain quiet
has set in, like a tired traveler
who nods off in a musty room.
A plush red theater known for melodrama
has shut down for good.

Today in the garden after a night of spring rain,
recalling my father,
whose birthday it would have been,
I hear the miniscule migrant kinglet sing
for the first time ever in this spot,
a warm wind roaring like surf.
The redbud's suddenly studded magenta.
The kinglet flashes the scarlet of his crown,
a tiny crest, a tiny strip, a tiny vivid
slash like blood, and I find myself
weeping as much for what is
as what's gone.

Epitaphs

The oak savannah is long gone,
replaced by farmland and a highway
that has spawned a maze of offshoots:
Timber Ridge Trail, Green Clover Court,
Wood's Edge Road. They always name
what they are taking.

Each year another street, another squad
of houses, soon to be flanked by offices.
Here, last year's fields have sprouted
Pinnacle Fitness and Health; ACH Business
Suites; an orthodontist's. Beyond,
a concrete path leads to a heap of dirt
topped by a digger. The earth is flagged
with *For Sale* signs declaring: *Build
to Suit,* there's *Space Available.*

One small farm remains.
Veal calves lying in hutches
surrounded on two sides by housing,
on the third by road.
Beyond, the new Savannah Oak
Elementary School, whose US flag droops
in the windless air.

A black expanse of parking space
covers the earth beneath.

Still, Life

the Antarctic ice shelf just lost
        a chunk   seven times as big as Manhattan
            if you live in America
my land by emigration

in Britain   the land of my birth
        that chunk was the Isle of Man

in Spain   my land by adoption
        it was the province of Burgos

to feel loss   we have to make it local
        the globe   our yard

once   as a child   I saw a Portuguese man-of-war
        drifting downwind   mauve caravel
in pristine waters   off the Outer Hebrides
        but now my screen predicts the Gulf
Stream that hugs the British Isles
        could stray   plunging the kingdom into a new
            Ice Age

last year I saw twelve storks trying to nest on one church tower
       in old Castile   no longer
            migrating south to Africa

but winter here on the Great Lakes was so hard the squirrels
        gnawed the bark from the small high branches
ice dammed on eaves and melted into ceilings
        highways   became rutted village lanes
and icicles   hazardous to passing humans

the recently emerged yards
        are muddy as flood-grounds
spring has come violent here
        this week I saw a home   lurch
whole and entire   into a brown   maelstrom
        and break apart   roof upside down

                a shipwrecked ark

Good Friday in the Department of Natural Resources

Because despite it all dove-note, leaf-mold, fox-stink, char-smell
and thin crazed ice in early-morning puddles

Because toothwort, trout lilies, aconite
and squill have elbowed their way skyward

Because winter's drab finches are newly lemonbright
and frog choirs creak from hidden bogs

Because the first returning warblers flash their yellow rumps
in the bare trees by the spring

Because from the blackened prairie
green shoots are rising, born of fire

Because the soilbound eggs of this June's grasshoppers
will soon become nymphs, instar after instar

Because this rifled earth can somehow still
spin gold from last year's straw

Mayday Manifesto

Let the planting wait,
and the scrubbing and raking and weeding.
Let no mulch be applied.
Let the lawns not be mowed: let the sweet grass
flower for once. Let no beds be dug,
let earth do what it will.
Let exams be unwritten,
untaken, ungraded. Let the files be unopened,
the emails unanswered, the folders stay folded.
Let's shed all our backpacks and burdens.
Let our backs be unstooped and our stoops
be much sat on. Let's grow fat and fecund.
Let wanton and wild be law.
Let's saunter and loiter. Let's hail our neighbors
and note how we're all a shade older.
Let's linger on sidewalks in small-talk.
Let's inhale the air with abandon,
take long swigs of lilac.
Let crab-apple trees leave us speechless.
Let's stroke their dark bark, press our faces to blossom.
Let's remember, remember
how long we have waited for this.
Let moles follow their noses,
let the chipmunks refashion their chambers.
Let the robins and wrens raise their young.
Let redwings take over the world.
Let weeds sprout from the cracks in the concrete,
the fox feast on chicken, the coyotes roam and guffaw.
Let the orioles weave their pendular nests
way up high, darting and flashing.
Let the redstarts be raucous and various.
Let the young maple put out its leaves and grow tall.
Let its taproot reach deep.

Let the fern fronds uncoil into plumes.
Let ants trace the turgid, rotund
buds of peonies, sucking their sap.
Let heat come, and rain.
Let magnolias drop all their clothes.
Let's stand still and listen, just listen,
trying to name every song.

Vouchsafed

It's been a somber day, deaths rising. On the road this morning: one traffic-flattened leopard frog; one squashed chipmunk, oozing crimson; one painted turtle, its carapace perfectly intact, not crushed by the car wheel, but framed by its own pink and grey guts. Glancing out the window during a lull in the rain, I am baffled by a commotion in the sumac bush: a ruby-throated hummingbird is ducking and diving amongst the leaves, rolling its throat, breast and belly over them as if swimming on the wing. A chickadee joins in. Suddenly, I realize the two of them are leaf-bathing in the leftover raindrops. They are too tiny to use the birdbath. I am suffused with delight.

Postcard from Washington Island, Wisconsin

I came here hoping to forget the drought, wildfires, floods. But Lake Michigan, too, is angry and navy, the waves edged with white spume under a slate-colored sky. The car ferry spews dark smoke as it hauls its cargo of *Homo sapiens* and vehicles back and forth across Death's Door. The rain is never-ending. "Welcome to my pond," the landlady says bitterly, surveying her waterlogged lawn. The lake keeps rising. Monarchs still flutter helplessly across it, wind-battered, trying to head south. All night, the sky gods hurl the furniture of heaven. The next morning, the beach is littered with tattered monarchs, mostly motionless, exhausted or dead. I spot one that is still stirring, move it carefully to a more sheltered spot amid the dune grass. Maybe the sun will warm it. As if that tiny act of propitiation could matter to the spirits of earth, air, water. A gesture that small, that elementary, that inadequate.

Maple in October

An angel
this tree
wings
luminous with leaves

burning on a black
menorah

A reaper
this wind
blade
honed keen

come to
blow them out

It is December and we must be brave

about the warmth more than the cold, the lilacs
lured into half-bloom, little mauve stubs.

December heat raised beads of sap from our front door.
Felled forty years ago, its xylem still keeps rising.

The cold, when it comes, can kill you. Months overdue,
the mercury plunges overnight.

All the ginkgos in the city drop their leaves
in synchrony, stepping out of their frilly saffron frocks.

*

I wake in the night to the scent of winter air
forced through a crack in the window, blind rattling.

Wind on the rampage, roaring like a vengeful god
unappeased by raking, by our bright and jeweled lights.

When it drops, the world seems to hold
its breath in the iron stillness before snow.

A frost-numbed lacewing toils along the windowsill
doing what it knows to do the only way it can.

*

Over the swarms of masked and unmasked
students, an atrium of sky, achingly blue.

A sweet, wild call, musical, strange, harsh, new:
tundra swans flown south in search of open water.

Remember summer's thimbleberries, how small
and soft, their flavor ghosted in your mouth?

Remember the way worms move, a contraction passing
through them, the way you pull elastic

through a tight space for a drawstring:
bunching, ruching, then releasing, easing forward?

Aldo Leopold's "On a Monument to the Pigeon": An Erasure

We
                                            grieve

                                    a living wind
            the   oaks   remember

There will   be
    effigies
    Book-pigeons   not
                wings

Our grandfathers
                                        bettered their lot

            man
    the sole object

        one species

                              slew

                                      the last

                            pigeons

    this wide valley
               will watch
clearer, colder, lonelier

                    the firmament
went out

                To love what *was* is a new thing

Disappearing the Birds

> *Bye-bye Birdies: Almost 3 Billion Birds [have]
> Disappeared from North America's
> Skies in Less Than 50 Years.*
>   Forbes headline, Sep 23, 2019

Disappeared sounds so innocuous—
fault-free and absolved of agency.

When birds die, they like to do it
secretly. It's rare to see their bodies;

even a holocaust of billions leaves
no mark, no mounds of carcasses.

Unseen—that's the problem.
No public mourning, absence

an open wound. Which is why
I still remember the cedar waxwing

I found dead on the asphalt outside
a new parking garage. Killed

by colliding with the glass-walled stairwell.
The gut-punch of grief: its small, buff

body, masked and crested, a buttercup-
yellow band across its tail. Cradling

its still-warm corpse in my hands,
I recalled flocks of cedar waxwings

in the aspens by a stream-fed lake
in Canada. Their piccolo notes shrilled

all day long for two golden weeks
one summer, a high faerie sound woven

through and over the rush and din
of running water. I thought, naively,

that they'd always be there,
looked for them in later years,

but they never came again.

Unseasonable

heat spawned 50 tornadoes down south,
razing whole towns, a candle factory,
an Amazon warehouse
death upon death

it sounded like a train came through the building

further south the Amazon burns and burns
while dark-blue Amazon vans patrol
the neighborhoods like paddy wagons,
their drivers often lost and shabby,
never the same from week to week,
expendable, disposable
as plastic, cardboard

Wisconsin & Southern Railroad
freight cars thunder at intervals
through this city, hauling "forest
products," corn, soy, fertilizers,
road-building aggregate, sheetrock,
frac sand, ethanol, liquid petroleum

one block away, two giant new homes are rising,
braat braat of nailgun, screwgun,
stapling, hammering,
cement drum grinding out its grey

three houses down, the roar of chainsaws
as a giant spruce is first beheaded
then debranched, stumped and ground down
all day long

a 102-year-old man believes that Covid
was Gaia trying to rid herself of us
next time, he says,
she will try harder

Sermon from the Marsh

Forget Christ. In the beginning it was Muskrat who died for us,
floating up drowned, clutching his pawful of world-making mud.
His small, limp body warned there's no returning for the dead,
no mystic resurrection for the animals, only the Son of Man,
who keeps on multiplying and subduing, who has dominion
over every living thing in the waters, air, and earth. Forget
the Pilgrims, too. In the beginning was the fur trade,
the voyageurs, advance guard of the long invasion that led
to trains, cars, tractors, diggers, dams, developments and
Departments of Natural Resources that named the muskrats
"furbearers," as if their use to us was all they are—millions
still trapped by hobbyists each year, more for the fun
than money, each pelt nowadays worth just a couple bucks.
Yet their dead bodies fed us once and clothed us in warm hats.
So, blessed be the furbearers, whose skins helped found America.

Blessed be the peace-mongers, signaling all-clear by swimming
their chevrons across the lakesilk when the land-lumberers
have passed. Blessed be their small heads ferrying steadily
to and fro, rudders undulating in the dusking quiet. Blessed
be the secretive and wary, for they may live long enough to mate.
Blessed be the survivors who ply the creeks, rivers, marshes,
ponds, and ditches, who dig their dens with hidden underwater
portals accessed only from below. Blessed be their lust, his musk
of rotten apples and fermented fish; her milksweet fertility.
Blessed be the water they couple in unseen, shuddering
together. Blessed be their all-consuming hunger, the gloopy
strands of pondweed they draw up, deft as magicians
pulling endless green scarves from their hats, their focus
and precision as they guzzle, as if slurping noodles from a bowl.

Blessed be the sustaining shoots, roots and rhizomes:
arrowhead, lily, cattail, milfoil, bullrush, duck potato, iris,
sedge. Blessed be the mire, the rank, rich mud and algae,
and blessed be lake-depths flecked with grains of pollen
fired by sun-shafts. Blessed be the ice that holds the muskrats'
ragged winter shelters, and the breakup of the ice, the grit
and sleet and raw before the twilight arias of robins,
the daylight churrs of scores of redwing blackbirds.
Though they will never inherit this earth, blessed
be the humble muskrats, for theirs is the kingdom
of shrinking wetlands and the glory of murky waters,
before the warming seas rise up once more.

II

The Naturalist, July 2020

Fear grips his heart in its mailed fist and squeezes—
        so hard, sometimes, he cries out.
                Contagion stalks us all, some
      more than others. Those who can't Zoom
from home, those, for example,
        with scores of coworkers, none
                of whom wear masks.
      We all have to breathe.
So many colors to depict the vicious orbs,
        the spiked spheres, like space invaders—
                red and blue, of late, the electron
microscope technicians' go-to hues.
Weekends, he soothes himself
        by searching for insects, the tinier
                the better. Magnified by his zoom
      lens, the minute becomes miraculous,
multifarious, becomes what can sustain us
        as the tiny maces of the novel virus
                wreak their wreckage in the world.

Mating Red Milkweed Beetles
Tetraopes tetrophthalmus

The Lovers

What are you looking at?
You jealous or what? Piss off and leave us alone.
You can call us "Four Eyes" all you want.
It no longer stings. We've found
each other. We're the colors
of love and death. Death especially.
We ate roots all winter to survive.
Rebirthed ourselves in earthen chambers.
Severed the veins of toxic sap upstream
before tucking in. We haunt scrubland
and verges looking for milkweeds' stout,
rebellious stems, those few
not yet Rounded Up like all the others.
If you only knew to listen,
you might hear us purr.

Green Coneheaded Planthopper
Acanalonica conica

The Lovers

What are you looking at?
You jealous or what? Piss off and leave us alone.
You can call us "Four Eyes" all you want.
It no longer stings. We've found
each other. We're the colors
of love and death. Death especially.
We ate roots all winter to survive.
Rebirthed ourselves in earthen chambers.
Severed the veins of toxic sap upstream
before tucking in. We haunt scrubland
and verges looking for milkweeds' stout,
rebellious stems, those few
not yet Rounded Up like all the others.
If you only knew to listen,
you might hear us purr.

Green Coneheaded Planthopper
Acanalonica conica

Green, I Love You Green

We cannot see her, living
leaf among the living leaves.
Yet she sees us. She
and her kind have been here
since the Eocene.

She can spring like a flea,
skedaddle crabwise, forwards, back,

yet prefers to walk slow,
peacefully feeding on phloem,
sipping cell sap for the sweet.
Secreter of nectar, maker of manna,
a scrim of venous green, suffused
from within by a chlorophyll sun.

Small ants tend her young
in teams. Like anxious hairdressers,
they stroke, pat, and fuss over them,
insistent, solicitous, milking the babes'
honeydew, efficiently farming
their charges, even when grown.

This leaf can see.
She wants us to leave.

Buffalo Treehopper Nymph
Stictocephala bisonia

Nymph

> *Nymph, in thy orisons*
> *Be all my sins remember'd.*
> > —Hamlet

Tree-sprite, sap-sipper, woodshrimp, locust-lover,
of one substance with the green you feast on,
weird wee beastie with twin rows
of saplings sprouting from your back;
striped translucence, skyfacing embryonic bison
at your inscrutable and beautiful orations, pray
for the remission of my sins, my miniature
Insectageddons: that plastic gallon
of pyrethrin that I sprayed around
our one small cherry tree to slay
the bronze-green-shielded beetles
busily devouring its leaves—
and after, noticing the beebalm
full of honeybees below; the
Ant Killer I still dole out in viscous globs
of murderous ambrosia they flock to,
thinking it a gift, signaling each other,
pressing shoulder to shoulder in a ring
to feed; the can of foaming
Wasp and Hornet Killer that I bought,
shamed, knowing what I did,
and coward that I was, aimed the nozzle
at a mud daubers' nest from twenty feet away.
The hiss, fizz, jet of extinguishment,
the hive-hum silenced in a second,
only the scent of evil on the air, and after,
the sound of pale foam dripping
floorwards from the porch ceiling,
all the quiet dead enshrouded in it.

Blinded Sphinx Moth Caterpillar
Paonia excaecata

Hornworm

One day I will fly by night,
hornworm turned
hummingbird.
Believe it. But
I was never blind—
you got that wrong.
No one put out my eyes.
I've twelve of them. All
I need to see is light and how
it changes. Horned though
I am, I'm innocent
as a unicorn. Soft. Green.
Voracious. Five, six
times I'll eat enough
to split my skin and crawl
out larger, hungrier.
Be fooled. Be fearful
of me, take my fierce-
looking rear for front.
I am insatiable because
one day I'll have
no mouth at all.

Apache Jumping Spider
Phidippus apacheanus

Stowaway

When the naturalist spies her
scaling his apartment wall, he suspects
she hitched a ride here on his gear
ten days ago. He remembers
finding one just like her—a rare
sight, this far north—and leaning
close to her lichen-spotted rock
in a failed attempt to take her picture.
But here she is, the size of a rice grain
in peacock and flame, no longer
the witnessed but the witness.
Her eight eyes see him in the UV
spectrum, colors he cannot perceive.

She spins, not webs, but silken tents,
Arabian princess who overnights
in hidden places, under sunflower leaves
or logs. Sun-lover, daytime hunter,
she stalks and pounces on her prey.
If she came alone, she will die here
alone; no more suitors to woo her
with flamenco dances, forelegs raised
above their heads, swaying and singing
their rumble-song, circling
her gingerly, eager as matadors,
though she is the lethal one.
She may stab and eat spurned lovers
if she so please.

He builds her a cardboard studio,
puts in a piece of petrified
wood for her to crawl on, takes
all the photos she would not permit
before, on her home turf. Then,
tenderly, bears her outside
to be released, wishes her well,
wishes her safe overwintering.

Cherry-Faced Meadowhawk
Sympetrum internum

Cherry-Faced Meadowhawk

Small carnivore soaking up late sun,
is that a ruby or a bloodspot on your wings?

As our northworld tilts toward the dark,
you weave air and gold October light

with your scarlet spindle, your slim
wand that's spun and spun inimitable spells

through eons of lost time, primeval
aviator, here before the birds, before

the dinosaurs. Your stigmata are not
wounds, but mystic marks of grace.

You snatch your few short weeks
of bliss, fighting and mating on the wing,

trapeze artist decked in cherry goggles
while the leaves loose and release

themselves, locusts' ocher minnows,
ashes' wine-dark ovals, October

with all its losses, trees' great galleons
ablaze, while all along the globe

spins and spins around the sun, regardless
of the gouts of blood, canary, flame,

the flocks of leaves scudding and drifting
like snow that's all too soon to come.

Meantime, you bask in the slant sun's
last life-giving sweetness as I

feast upon your fire-engine red, infuse
it into my bones to tide me through.

Dog-Day Cicada
Neotibicen canicularis

Cicadas

I landed in Wisconsin that first time in the dog days of summer, sultry and humid and reverberant with sound. The very air was singing like the sea, great cyclical surges that emerged out of the trees, rose, peaked, and faded in a hypnotic pattern that resembled the long, slow inhale-hold-exhale-hold of meditation, the deep calm when the mind quiets and consciousness floats on the swells of breath. That first season in America I was lonely, dazed, disoriented, mateless, not knowing my mate was out there, looking also, or that we'd arrived here on the selfsame day. Sirius, the Dog Star, rose invisibly in the unfamiliar, exotic dawns. I had to learn about bug screens, not to leave doors ajar or open unscreened windows. Meanwhile the male cicadas kept on singing in the trees, the drill of their lust piercing the somnolent afternoons, each one broadcasting his coordinates over and over to the universe, lighthouse beams circling rhythmically over the emptiness. I sometimes found their husks on the sidewalk, little sarcophagi of missing Pharaohs. It would be years before I found an actual body and marveled at the stout, ancient-looking creature, its bullish head and huge eyes, its black tail and woodland camo above, an army uniform improbably topped with extra-long see-through wings, their transparent panels separated by an intricate tracery of malachite-green veins, like a Tiffany lamp. The body blunt and homely, purpose-built for work and survival; the wings speaking of something else altogether. The little ribbed organ on its vulnerable underside, like whale baleen but tiny, that in life flexes and shudders frenetically, a built-in vibrator. A hollow abdomen that acts as sounding board and amp for the message, "Come to me and we'll come together!"

Peacock Fly
Callopystromyia annulipes

Peacock Fly

Tiny peacock strutting your stuff on a rotten
log, dear smidgeon of stonefish, dear bug-eyed

fleck of animate female granite encrusted
with creekbed crud and sequined in sapphires,

your courtship dance is entrancing the male
you have your eye on, bejeweled like you

and doing semaphore with his matching patchwork
fans as he do-si-dos, the two of you gender-equity

eaters of detritus, mutual choosers of mates.
May the wrens and the tanagers spare you

today till the dance is done and your eggs
are laid, that the dance may go on.

Red-banded Leafhopper
Graphocephala coccinea

Leafhopper Search

     Blink. Look closer. A common
What are leafhoppers and how do I get rid of them?
     milkweed leaf holds you, sliver
Are leafhoppers good or bad?
     of cerulean slashed with scarlet,
Do leafhoppers bite humans?
     bright as a tropical fish or hyacinth
Are leafhoppers invasive?
     macaw, but no exotic, perfectly at home, perfect-
Are leafhoppers toxic?
     ly innocuous to plants and beasts.
What repels leafhoppers?
     You unspeech me. Such profligate color
How do I keep leafhoppers off my plants?
     in your speck of life, such consummate
What kills leafhoppers organically?
     design—why? How? And what
Will soapy water kill leafhoppers?
     in the world
What is the best insecticide to kill leafhoppers?
     have I been doing,
We'll nix what's pestering you.
     not to have known
How to get rid of leafhoppers in 4 simple steps.
     you till now?

Acorn Weevil
Curculio glandium

Acorn Weevil

Midsummer
high on the Tree: your mother,
freshly fucked, strokes a young green acorn
with her dowsing-rod antennae, divines the precise spot,
saws a pinhead circle through the pericarp with the blades
on her exquisitely curved rostrum, quaffs the kernel's rich
oil, and then drills deep, steady and deep, reaching up to her
hilt into its oaken heart. Turning, she posts a pearled egg
down the shaft, plugs it with dung to disguise it. Oh to be
bounded in a nutshell, your orb   your ark   your abbey,
feasting on the fruit of the Tree, the nut your nursery and
you curled creamy nestled nuzzling   gnawing. Your
darksecret love ecstatic. Come Fall the acorn, your larder-
fortress, falls. Together, you never fall far from the Tree.
Percussion of impact your cue to chew a hatch out of the
hold, then wriggle struggle your pillowy amplitude effort-
fully through—you have ballooned after all that eating—
tumble onto oakleaf duff and grub down into the soil at
the Tree's roots to drowse, dream, dissolve and recast
yourself for years—one, two, five—till one warm
day you stir, clamber out, lift your unused elytra,
unfold your long tulle wings, still creased
with newness, and fly up to the Tree
from which you came to begin
again

Ghost Tiger Beetle
Cicindela lepida

Praying to the God of Small Things

The naturalist is on his knees, head
to the ground, rump in the air
as if in Child's Pose, his absorption
a kind of adoration. He is
prostrate for his devotions,
praying to the god of small things.

In the background, the Wisconsin
slides by lazily, bright as burnished
tin the June sun strikes
hard with the flat of its sword.
Heat rises from the beach
in small, sight-warping dervishes
that spiral skyward. This stretch
of river-sand seems empty
but is not. It is the haunt
of monsters, alive with ticking,
flying, leaping, murder:

Ghost Tiger Beetles, smallest
of their clan, ferocious, visible
mainly by their shadows.
Pearlescent speedsters,
they stalk by fits and starts,
running so fast their vision
(and the watcher's) blurs,
bowling along like seed tufts
blowing over sand. Ant-eaters,
fly-catchers, they are solitary
and secretive, often ambushing
their prey from burrows,
wielding their scimitared
mandibles.

                    Just when he has one
in focus, it flits. Fearless,
it scoots into his human shade
to cool itself, standing
high on its stilted legs,
away from the burning earth.

Each year into insect
Armageddon, even the Ghosts,
he says, are fewer.

Porcelain Gray Moth
Protoboarmia porcelaria

Whisper, Universe, Eclipse

The above are collective names for a group of moths. There were 1,284 species of moths left in Wisconsin as of 2018, including the following:

Your names are nocturnes,
encyclopedias of wonder—

moonseed   milkweed tussock   snowberry sphinx   dappled dart
    gooseberry barkminer   confused woodgrain
                     rosewing
little white lichen   toadflax brocade   scalloped sallow

For each tree and plant, a moth—
or more than one—exquisitely
evolved to dwell on it.

variegated midget   ruby quaker   cloaked marvel
   pickerelweed borer   black-bordered lemon
        waterlily leafcutter linden looper

Soft, soft furred,
gentle, bumbling, blurred—
without you, no wild silk.

white flannel   American ermine   arched hooktip
    tufted apple-bud   Baltimore snout
   corn earworm   abbreviated button

Drab dryads,
noctilucent innocents,
you flourish in the dark.
There, you are flamboyant.

pearly wood-nymph   oldwife underwing   chinquapin leafminer
    basswood leafroller   purple carrotseed   green pug
      pistachio emerald   harnessed tiger

I have never seen a Luna.
May never, now.

promiscuous angle   afflicted dagger
      adjutant wainscot   *forgotten frigid owlet*

Going, going, gone.
A whispering universe, eclipsing,
soon to be eclipsed.

The Fog Harvesters

*after an image of a Flying Saucer Trench Beetle
by Levon Biss in his Microsculpture exhibit*

Snagged in my mind like flotsam
on river willows at high water—
the beetles of the Namib Desert
who live on less than half an inch
of rain a year. On nights when fog
rolls in from the Skeleton Coast,
Flying Saucer Trench Beetles dig
tiny trenches on the slip face of dunes,
slurp dew pearls that gather on the ridges.
Others—the Darklings—station themselves
in Downward Dog, basking
heads down in the sand, backs facing
up into the fog-bearing wind,
to sip slow condensation as it trickles
down their elytra to their mouths.

*

Snagged or smashed on the summer
windscreens of our childhood—when
did it stop?—hundreds of dancing
insects, interrupted. That golden air.
The emptying air. The ever-more-
empty air.

*

At the crane zoo, all the world's
fifteen species of crane are gathered
in separate pens on restored prairie,

labeled *Vulnerable. Threatened. Critically
Endangered.* Early August and all
the native grassland plants are blooming—
but in two hours we see only three
butterflies: one Cabbage White,
one Swallowtail, one Monarch.

*

Some moths have sound receptors tuned
to the pitch of bats' hunting screams,
can hear them from thirty yards and take
evasive action.

*

Bumblebees—there are two dozen
species in Wisconsin—like to nest
in chipmunk burrows.

*

Is this ode or elegy?

*

One quarter of the creatures on the planet is a beetle.

*

Nabokov—compulsive lepidopterist—wrote
I confess I do not believe in time.

He thought the world, so full of butterflies
and moths, *a continuous shimmer of . . . wings*
when he was young, would always be so. Loved
their death spasms, the *satisfying crackle*
of pin penetrating thorax, each specimen
lusted after, hunted, mounted.
Sometimes, he says, *I caught*
the subtle perfume of butterfly wings
on my hands, a perfume that varies
with the species; it may be vanilla,
or lemon, or musk . . . So many
shared his greed, his kink,
children let loose in paradise
with nets and killing jars.

*

This island is infested with Brazilians,
the old man said. By which he meant
overrun with vermin. By which he meant,
swarming like insects, like roaches.
By which he meant, teeming with aliens.
By which he meant invasives.

*

Invasive: that's us. We're the invasives.

*

Yet every insect image Levon Biss creates
derives from unimaginable attention—
in other words, a kind of tenderness. For each,

he took eight thousand portraits of a single corpse
from the Oxford Museum of Natural History.
which holds over seven million insect specimens
from every country in the world. Darwin, Wallace—all
the great Victorian collectors' loot is stored there,
records of prelapsarian abundance.

*

I will never visit the Namib Desert. But the thought
of those beetles milking the fog—what can I say?
Earth is inconceivably plural. And the fog, those few nights
it arrives, must taste something like mercy.

III

Desert Soliloquy

Summer Lake, Oregon

Frost has sweetened the apples and the black bears come down
from the hills to eat them.

The stars are all around us. They even touch the ground.

Humans have been coming here for 15,000 years. The old ones left
their sandals. They walked here from the sea.

Shhh. The rattlesnakes are sleeping.

The sky lies down on the long flanks of the hills and looks
at its face in the glass.

The trees are few, bare and unmoving. To live here, you need
a deep taproot.

Two birds fly into the radiance. No wind stirs.

The water comes and goes. When it vanishes, the mud cracks.
The lake's parched lips turn white.

I came here to be emptied, filled

With silence.

Thanksgiving at Indian Ford Meadow

Sisters, Oregon

Minute by minute, dawn's dim light
      intensifies, as if something very powerful
           were focusing its gaze.

Step outside into that clarifying
      light, the shutters of your heart
           flung wide from within.

Wend your way through the Ponderosas ringing
      the meadow, silent watchtowers whose canyoned
           bark smells of smoke.

Enter the sagebrush, wild rye, bluebunch wheatgrass,
      yarrow and rabbitbrush, each blade and flowerhead
           aflash with frost's pinprick firedots.

The very earth here was birthed by fire, lava-
      froth cooled into scoria, long since time-scoured
           into red-grit soil and pumice-rubble.

Milky glass lids the frozen hollows underfoot.
      The bleached blond steppes speak the slow
           language of the sacred, the gold

grasses haloed in a contained radiance,
      as if lit from within by all the suns
           of their lifetimes.

Four Collects

Annunciation

First shoals of locust leaves
heaped in windrows,
drifts of gold in the gutter.

Absolution

Midday moon's communion
wafer floats, dissolving,
in a sea of blue.

Transubstantiation

Winter, mid-morning—
a carpet of stars,
a galaxy underfoot.

Epithalamium

June rainstorm scatters
linden-blossom bracts, lime-green
wildworld confetti.

Self-Portrait as Yellow Warbler

after Aimee Nezhukumatathil

      Let me glimpse your green shadows

at dawn   tender cover

          shield me close

     in your shimmering thicket   I'm faint

famished   and dying to flit   in your catkins

     sally-gleaning   to feast on your bugs

Look for me always   near water   sunsplinter

    I was born to this northern light

and it's reeled me back   between worlds

    I left after dusk   alone   one of millions

I've flown thousands of miles   all at night

              Ask me   about the gulfs

   I've covered   the accents   I've acquired

When I beg for more sweet   lavish me with larvae

     soused on honeysuckle scent

   These blood streaks on my chest   I'm still healing

will always   bear scars   I could nest

      in your crotch   your strong   steady stems

proffer you my cup   raise

          at last   my brood

No Matter How Full

after meals I crave something sweet.
This wanting always.
I peel a mandarin, feed myself its fragrance.
Outside it's been raining all day. Fog
bloomed mysteriously at dusk, blotting out
the dripping trees, the hillside with its swords of switchgrass.
Earlier, a handsome grey bird I didn't recognize.
Only when he took to the air did I see the blue
cascade, his jay-wings splaying like a fan.
We talk on the phone. You're disarmingly easeful.
On the mantel the miniature jeweled frame—
blue, ruby, fuchsia—holding a diminutive you,
dimpled, in a white onesie. How absolutely
I loved you then—still do—from my core.
You, amiable even in utero.
Did I give you enough? Will I bequeath
you my grief? *Compatible* comes from Latin:
suffer with. Suffering seeps, and sometimes
I long to die. To float away,
to become air. But you're my ballast.
There's no leaving now.

Empty Nest Ghazal

Spring is advancing crabwise, by degrees, first fast then slow.
I measure time by the departing snow.

The trees are bare and leafless, still, as if shell-shocked.
A few hold nests that have survived the winter's winds and snow.

I found a small one, fallen, that I've kept.
Woven of grass and lined with willow fluff, it's cup-shaped, low.

The spring migration has begun. The robins have returned.
The loons are back, and male red-wings conk-la-reeing to and fro.

It was time, I know. You were readying to fledge.
When the sandhill cranes came bugling, it was your turn to go.

I expected it would be much worse, being without you.
Just a stab or two a day. Your leaving wasn't such a blow.

But sometimes I dream I'm nursing you again,
my breasts heavy with the milk that wants to flow.

Such happiness back then when you were on my hip,
exhausted but content with you in tow.

I must unlearn, relearn the name for mother, sleep more deeply.
Let you go. I'll measure time by the departing snow.

Wisconsin Honey

Aztec gold
sungod-given
liquid amber
nectar lava
worker-stored
in waxy cells
in glowing jars
on shelves
each jar distilled
from 72,000
miles of flight
crunch and melt
the sharp sweetness
of flowers
pumpkin
linden blossom
thyme
I spread my bread
with sunlight

Dance Floor

On the woodland path, one branch of the beech sapling ahead is covered in snow. In Indian summer. No. It is moving. Cottonwood fuzz, milkweed fluff, stirs in the breeze. No. Look again. The branch's fur twitches. Step closer, to eye height. Squint. Try to make sense of the nonsensical. The branch is ajiggle not with snow or seeds but a host of tiny, almost translucent bugs that raise and lower their rear ends at random intervals like jittery scorpions. Instead of a sting, they brandish something resembling miniature feather dusters. They remind you of those madly disheveled troll dolls from the 90s, but these up-combed shocks of snowy floss are interspersed with incongruous long, white filaments. Because their movements are not synchronized, the effect is perplexing. Each miniature insect flourishes its bushy tail like a truce flag. *Don't eat me! I'm not food! I am waxy white fluff—not worth your while.* The branch dances, each bug shaking its little booty for all it is worth. Bafflement turns to disbelief turns to delight. How not to worship a world in which beech aphids boogie? How not to be humbled, how not to get high on the sheer goddamn weirdness of this world?

Schoolhouse Beach, Washington Island, Wisconsin

Turn your back
on the one-room schoolhouse
closed long ago. Descend
through the graveyard, its plastic flags,
its plastic flowers. Don't spare
them a glance. Gaze
straight ahead, into the dark
grove before you, the road's
end, downhill. And then—
out of the blue—through
the louvers of cedars, blue
blindsides you, heartlifts you,
bowls you over. Blue in all
its moods: peacock, Prussian,
Aegean, robin's egg, teal, aqua,
lapis, verdigris, sloe.
A steep-shelving shore, its white
stones softened and smooth.
A steamship lies dreaming
18 feet down, its oak
keelsons splintered,
hull holed, drift-pins
crusted with mussels.
8 November, 1913:
snow, the Big Blow.
At night, boneblack
sky full of stars: the Dipper,
Cassiopeia, Orion,
the piercing lights of Venus
and Mars.

Triptych: A Book of Hours

Dawn

Into our bedroom's dark fug, before dawn,
for the first time in months, drift fragments of song.
A robin—just back—on the garage roof
threads this northern silence with notes.
Freezing drizzle, grey pall, the lawn piebald with snow—
but he's giving thanks. His three limpid phrases
of praise rise and fall, piercing my caul of sleep.
He's the bridegroom of half-light, of dream.
Wished-for as clean water, the bright drops of his song
stitch winter to spring. We're no longer alone—
His voice marries us, and this is his psalm:
to live is to give voice. All days are one.

Dusk

This is the time of shapeshifters. The skyline morphs
from peach to indigo. Raccoons materialize from drains.
Commuters in their carcoons course through the city's veins.
Houses exhale and stretch. Porch lights snap on.
The great blue heron flaps back to her roost. The barred owl
in the white pine blinks his yellow eyes, feels hunger stir.
A siren shrieks and from the shades, unseen coyotes keen:
a high, wild chorus to misfortune. This is the time when,
from the greenworld, deer appear, drifting like smoke,
to crop the grass with delicate precision. Shades
of the ancestors, haunting the perimeters of home.

Dark

There is so much to fear in the country of darkness.
You'll think you're sinking, you could founder in its waters,
that you'll vanish like a bright coin tossed in a well,
that you'll never swim back up or be recovered.
Know this: that one day you'll be found
up on the moors at midsummer, with curlews bubbling,
cupped in rainwater in the hollow of an ancient stone.
A boy will burnish you and keep you in his pocket.
The moon's bone ball swivels slowly in the socket of sky.
Night's a corrective, a necessary physic.
Only at night can you glimpse the history of distant stars.
Only at night can you see how small
and how accompanied you are.

Fish Out of Water

Late Christmas Day, a woman calls me:
she's seen bald eagles in the city.
Come with me, she says. Come to the lake.
You must see them.

New snow, an inch of down,
dry, weightless, floats on a world
scoured by a sub-zero wind.
The woods by the shore are monochrome.
Bald trees huddle, restive, resigned.
We traipse this way and that
along the point, wind in our faces,
making us weep. Nothing
but chickadees and crows.
The eagles have moved on.
But they have left a sign.

A fish on the path
in the oak leaves. Unmarked.
Exquisite. Plump. And frozen.
Every scale frozen, gills frozen, fins frozen,
frozen yellow eye. Pristine
and perfectly natural, this perch
here on the path, so
not a fish out of water.

Memento Mori

On the way back from a family funeral
twelve hundred miles away, I have a layover
at Chicago O'Hare, and scurrying through Concourse B
of Terminal 1 on the lookout for somewhere
to grab a bite to eat, I pass a dinosaur,
its gargantuan black skeleton looming
over me, its long, long neck reaching
the rafters of the domed glass ceiling,
gazing sightless at the planes parked on the tarmac,
and I know from *Jurassic Park* it's a brachiosaurus
though there's no plaque, no information
on where it came from, when it roamed this earth,
and no one stops or even seems to see it,
occupied as they are with making their flights,
putting their shoes on and liquids away after exiting
the security checkpoints with their X-
ray machines and packed conveyor belts,
the United terminal a hive of harried
humans and I stand under the creature's
Brobdingnagian ribs, so delicately curved and tapered,
think of it craning its neck to chomp the treetops,
disconsolate perhaps that they're not here, and peering
down at the pygmy shrew-sized mammals at its feet—
its ribs now holding air and space that once held muscle,
sinew, lungs, a massive heart—this small-skulled
herbivore, peacefully cropping the forests
whose foliage and trunks compacted for billennia became
the coal that fired our industry, the steel,
steam power, trains, that opened up the West, the world
all for our taking, so now we jet in mere hours
over oceans, burning the sludge of oceans past,

black like the painted reproduction of these bones
unearthed a century ago, our flying powered by fossil
fuels, the very thing we passengers are all engaged in
the reason why we're fated to be swallowed up
by fire and floods, wiped out as surely
as the dinosaurs, yet here we are, hastening our end,
heedless of the skeleton's stark message,
and I reflect upon this fact later at a writers'
retreat it takes me half a tank of gasoline
to reach, in a library with wing-backed chair
beneath a black and loudly ticking clock.

To Have But Not to Hold

You can splurge on a box of champagne
mangos trucked up from Mexico, gorge
in complicit bliss on their honey-lush flesh.
You can thrill to the wood thrushes' flutes,
hushed in what's left of the thickets,
each last note vibrating like a spring-
board after the diver has leapt.
Small survivors, hymning peace
to a soundtrack of traffic and backhoes.
Burning natural gas, you can steam
fat asparagus spears from Black Earth
that stink up your pee within minutes,
the greenworld's alchemy altering
you from within. You can witness
a host of primordial angels,
a hundred white pelicans migrating north
who descend on Lake Wingra
and stay for only a day, sporting weird
nuptial bumps on their saffron-bright bills.
You can drive miles each day
in pursuit of cerulean warblers,
rarer and rarer and not seen at all here
this year, but here is the black-throated blue,
and the azure flash of the bluebird's back.
You can mourn the small painted turtle
returning determined from trying
to lay her eggs on cement, then slipping
into the foamy green algae like silk.
You can greet the catbird, just back and meowing
for crabapple jelly, the furred tongues
of iris whose breath smells like grape.

You can save the small moth on the wall
from its torment of light and release
it to the darkling air. You can hold
your breath and sink to your knees
as two sandhill cranes and their cinnamon
colts stalk past, so close you can hear
the male purr, not with content
but alarm at your presence. You can
choose when to exit the ruinous cool
of your household AC, but you cannot
not breathe, not grieve the wildfire smoke
from up north—Nova Scotia, Alberta,
Saskatchewan—dimming the diamond-
sharp sky to a haze in mid-May, nor
fail to praise the green and the great
blue herons, side-by-side, motionless, almost
unseen on the island's far shore, nearing dusk.
So no, you can't hold onto any of it—
but for a moment you can have the ruby-
throated hummingbird thrumming by your side,
intent on the spray of precious, squandered
water glittering from your garden hose,
chittering his small call of reproof
        or delight.

Praise Song for a Plane Tree

For the plane tree (also known as
American sycamore) planted under
the direction of Aldo Leopold
on Arbor Drive, Madison, Wisconsin.

Heartstopper, thunderstriker,
piebald tree with the alabaster arms,
already you are ancient.
Even when young, you were in tatters.
You are husked, scabbed, leprous,
peeled and peeling, a fortress
in a sea of white snakeroot.
Like the brindled cat who visits every day,
you are chestnut and taupe, dun
and umber, antelope, parchment,
bone-marrow, pith.

You tell me to be at peace
with many names,
many skins, many strata;
to be a jumble of jigsaw pieces,
none of which fit, although all do.

Teach me to be pregnant with myself,
my own becoming, to bear stretch marks,
striations, moving tectonic plates,
to slough myself piecemeal day
by day and never look back.

Teach me to be sinuous:
how to change direction,
go baroque when constrained
by the press of others.

Teach me that growth means shedding,
loss. So many daily losses.
It means standing shucked and naked
to the world, exposed to view,
but without shame, because aren't we all
dying, aren't we all beautiful?

Tree, speak to me in blotch and mottle,
dapple and darklight.
Arrest me, gentle me, teach
me to breathe.

Teach me also to be stubborn
when ravaged by hungry mouths,
to cultivate hope every spring
in the face of blight, new shoots
withering to witch's brooms.
Show me the ways my cracks
will be secured with spidersilk,
its latticework of light.

Windtree oceaning, earth-anchored
hub and holdfast, teach me
windshimmer, windseethe,
how to be windfirm.
Rainseeder, whisperer,
heatshield me, hearten and relieve me,
shade me, tent me, nestle
me unseen at your muscled

roots, brawny as hawsers. Endure,
endear me to you, who are my kith and kin.
Conceal me, heal me, cleanse
me. You, my commonweal,
my common wealth,
your breath my breath.

Bide your sweet, Cretacean time.
Abide with me.
School me in survival.
Teach me to broaden,
deepen, keep on
reaching for the light.
Oh forebearer, forgive
my oblivion. Outlast, outlive me.

Notes

The title "It is December and we must be brave" is a line from Natalie Díaz's poem "Manhattan is a Lenape Word."

About the Aldo Leopold erasure poem: as recently as the nineteenth century, the passenger pigeon was the most abundant bird in North America. John Muir describes "flocks streaming south in the fall so large that they were flowing from horizon to horizon in an almost continuous stream all day long." The largest recorded nesting site was in my state, Wisconsin, near Black River Falls in 1871. It covered 850 square miles, with some 136 million birds present. Yet the entire species was massacred in a very short time, driven to extinction in the wild in 1902 and in captivity in 1914. Aldo Leopold wrote this essay in 1947 for the dedication of the Passenger Pigeon Monument at Wyalusing State Park in western Wisconsin. At that time, there were still Americans who could remember having seen passenger pigeons in their childhood.

"Sermon From the Marsh" evokes Potawatomi and Ojibwe creation stories, which relate that when the world was covered with water, various animals tried diving down in search of earth to place on Turtle's back. All failed except Muskrat, who drowned in the attempt but surfaced with a pawful of mud that became Turtle Island (the world/North America).

In "The Lovers," the reader should know that red milkweed beetles' genus and species names are derived from the Ancient Greek for "four eyes," because they do indeed have four.

The title "Green, I Love You Green" is a translation of a line in "Romance sonámbulo," by Federico García Lorca, "Verde que te quiero verde."

"The Fog Harvesters" was written in response to an extraordinary photography exhibition, *Microsculpture: The Insect Portraits of Levon Biss,* which has been traveling the world since its inauguration in 2016 and came to Verona, Wisconsin in 2023. It features insects from Oxford University's Museum of Natural History collections, presented in nine-foot-high images of breathtaking beauty and complexity. The exhibit can be found online.

"Self-Portrait as Yellow Warbler" was influenced by Donald's Kroodsma's work in *The Singing Life of Birds,* showing that significant regional variations often exist in song across the same bird species. Thus, birds that cover long distances in migration, as these warblers do, encounter members of their species with different ways of vocalizing, akin to our notion of regional or national accents.

About the Author

Catherine Jagoe is an award-winning British American writer and translator whose poems have been featured on *The Writer's Almanac* and *Poetry Daily*. Her previous poetry collections include *Bloodroot* (2016), *News from the North* (2014), and *Casting Off* (2007). Her nonfiction has received a Pushcart Prize and a citation in *Best American Essays*. She is a contributor to Wisconsin Public Radio's *Wisconsin Life* series.

Read more of her work on her website:
www.catherinejagoe.com

www.ingramcontent.com/pod-product-compliance
Lightning Source LLC
Chambersburg PA
CBHW072049160426
43197CB00014B/2691